Contents

KU-523-336

Any words appearing in the text in bold, **like this**, are explained in the Glossary. You can also look out for them in the Word Bank at the bottom of each page.

The horses slow down as the road gets steeper. The **stagecoach** rocks as its wooden wheels bump over the ruts. The passengers inside sway as they talk about the danger on the road at the start of the 1800s.

Then it happens. A galloping horse flashes past. Dust flies off the road. A gun fires and the horses rear up. A masked face peers through the gun-smoke into the coach. Terrified eyes stare back. Everyone gasps.

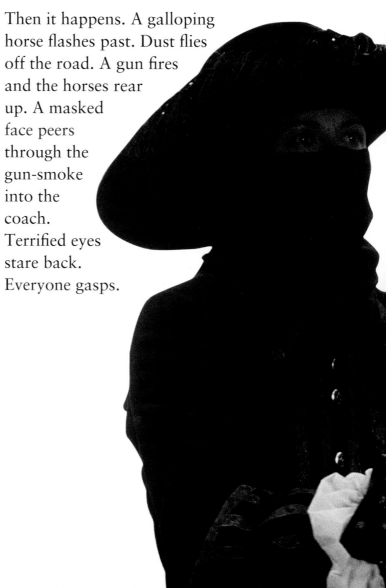

Robbing the rich

Most people think of outlaws as mysterious masked riders on horseback. They robbed the rich and sometimes even gave to the poor. They led exciting lives, and were brave and carefree. At least, that is how they might be seen now. In their day, outlaws were bad news!

Word Bank

outlaw robber on the run, wanted by the law enforcers

Items should be returned on or before the last date shown below. Items not already requested by other borrowers may be renewed in person, in writing or by telephone. To renew, please quote the number on the barcode label. To renew online a PIN is required. This can be requested at your local library.
Renew online @ **www.dublincitypubliclibraries.ie**
Fines charged for overdue items will include postage incurred in recovery. Damage to or loss of items will be charged to the borrower.

Leabharlanna Poiblí Chathair Bhaile Átha Cliath
Dublin City Public Libraries

Dublin City
Baile Átha Cliath

Central Library, Henry Street,
An Lárleabharlann, Sráid Annraoi
Tel: 8734333

Date Due	Date Due	Date Due

www.raintreepublishers.co.uk

Visit our website to find out more information about **Raintree** books.

To order:

☎ Phone 44 (0) 1865 888113

🖹 Send a fax to 44 (0) 1865 314091

💻 Visit the Raintree Bookshop at **www.raintreepublishers.co.uk** to browse our catalogue and order online.

First published in Great Britain by
Raintree, Halley Court, Jordan Hill, Oxford OX2 8EJ,
part of Harcourt Education.
Raintree is a registered trademark of Harcourt
Education Ltd.

Editorial: Melanie Copland
and Kate Buckingham
Design: Michelle Lisseter and Kamae Design
Picture Research: Maria Joannou and
Ginny Stroud-Lewis
Index: Indexing Specialists (UK) Ltd
Production: Duncan Gilbert

Originated by Dot Gradations Ltd
Printed and bound in China
by South China Printing Company

ISBN 1 844 43587 3 (hardback)
08 07 06 05 04
10 9 8 7 6 5 4 3 2 1

ISBN 1 844 43593 8 (paperback)
09 08 07 06 05
10 9 8 7 6 5 4 3 2 1

British Library Cataloguing in Publication Data
Townsend, John
Outlaws – (True Crime)
364.3

A full catalogue record for this book is available from
the British Library.

Acknowledgements
Corbis pp. 27, 39, 43, 24–25, 30–31, 38, 41
(Bettmann), 42 (Craig Aurness), 34, 44–45 (Harcourt
Index), 32 (Hugh Beebower), 9 (Lowell Georgia),
32–33 (Macduff Everton), 15 (Michael S Yamashita),
8 (Patrick Ward), 27 (Thom Lang); Corbis Sygma
p. 40 (John Van Hasselt); Hulton Archive pp. 42–43;
Kobal Collection pp. 16–17 (Touchstone/Marks,
Elliott); Mary Evans Picture Library pp. 10–11, 35;
Peter Newark's American Pictures pp. 21, 37, 13,
20–21, 20, 23, 28, 30, 31, 33; Peter Newark's
Historical Pictures pp. 16, 17, 18–19, 19; The Kobal
Collection/20th Century Fox pp. 7, 22, 38–39; The
Kobal Collection pp. 24 (Buster films/NHF Prods),
4–5, 9, (Cannon), 40–41 (Hollywood Pictures/
Cinergi), 12–13 (Icon Productions), 28–29
(Le Sac), 6–7 (Morgan Creek/Redin, Van), 14–15
(Orion), 34–35 (The Australian Film Commission/
Working Title/Johns, Carolyn); Topham Picturepoint
p. 12; Tudor Photography p. 26.

Cover photograph of hanging reproduced with
permission of Corbis/Bettmann

With a finger on the trigger and with a hint of a smile, the masked figure speaks just five words, 'Your money or your life'.

Dangerous travel

Highway robbery was once a real danger to travellers. In America in the 1800s, any robber who held up a stagecoach was called a road agent. In Australia, they were called bushrangers. A hundred years before, highwaymen attacked travellers in the UK and Europe. Even ships were not safe from robbers. Pirates could strike at any time. The world was at the mercy of the **outlaw**.

Outlaws were to be hunted down and killed. The law did not protect them from murder, because they chose to live outside the law. Most outlaws died young. They lived by the gun and died by the gun. It was their choice.

" Stand and deliver "

Find out later

Who was this feared pirate outlaw who lost his head?

Who had a $23,000 'dead or alive' reward on his head in the 1930s?

Who was Australia's most famous outlaw?

Robbers on the road

Bending the truth

Folktales grew and spread about many of the outlaws from history. This Australian song describes outlaws as brave:

Sons of Australia, forget not the brave, And gather wild flowers to place on their graves.

Tales of **outlaws** made great stories. People loved to talk about the exciting adventures of robbers, their escapes and chases, as well as their battles with the lawmen. As these stories were repeated down the years, the evil outlaws began to gain some respect. Instead of being selfish thieves, they became heroes who were kind to women and children. Stories twisted some of the truth.

The outlaw of **legend** was seen as fun, loyal to his friends and generous to the poor. He became the 'good badman' who fought against the rich and powerful. Fact turned into **fiction** – and outlaws became ideal characters for Hollywood films.

Jesse James in the middle in the 2003 film *American Outlaws*.

Word Bank

legend   story based on something real that may not be completely true

Violence or action?

Robbery is more than just stealing. It uses violence and force. It is always very cruel and shocking for the **victims**. Yet outlaws in many stories and films are often shown to be doing good by robbing. If the outlaw also saves a girl from danger and sweeps her up on his horse, he becomes the star of the film.

In the 1930s, film-makers were keen to show outlaws such as Jesse James in action. Films called '**westerns**' showed heroes and **villains** galloping across dusty plains. Film changed the image of the outlaw forever.

Robin Hood

Robin Hood is the most famous outlaw of legend in the UK. He was a skilled **archer** who robbed the rich and helped the poor in Sherwood Forest in the 12th century. In fact, there is no proof that Robin Hood ever existed. That has not stopped films (like above) being made about his life!

Highways

This diary written 300 years ago records how scary coach travel was:

The main roads are just muddy tracks. Coaches travel slowly from inn to inn, where we travellers stay overnight. It is easy to get lost because there are no maps of the roads and few signposts. Masked horsemen are often waiting. Our driver thinks they have spies in every inn, watching to see who is worth robbing.

Highway robbers

Bands of robbers roamed the UK and Europe for hundreds of years. The best place for their attacks was on the open road, where they could make a quick getaway.

Highwaymen

The **legends** of highwaymen started in the 17th century. In the stories, sons of rich gentlemen used to hold up coaches carrying wealthy people. This kind of highwayman worked alone, often wearing a mask and fine clothes. He was handsome and polite as he asked the ladies to hand over their jewels.

Although he waved a pistol, the gentleman highwayman rarely harmed his **victims**. In the real world, most highwaymen were no more than violent thugs.

Highwaymen were **notorious** in the 17th century. Some pubs are still named after them!

Word Bank

inn resting house for travellers, where they could eat and sleep overnight

Robbing with style

The Frenchman Claude Duval was known as the most charming highwayman ever to roam English roads. He would smile and lift his hat at the ladies he robbed. When he was arrested at an **inn**, many ladies pleaded with King Charles II to **pardon** him. Duval was hanged in 1670, aged 27.

Lady Catherine Ferrers (1662–84) was the young wife of a Lord. She was bored with her life and sneaked out at night to become a highway robber. She joined up with another highwayman. When he was caught and hanged, Catherine carried on alone but one night she was shot during a robbery. She staggered home and died.

The story of Lady Catherine has inspired films about highway-women.

Early death

Not many highwaymen survived beyond their early twenties. They were usually **betrayed** for a reward, called 'blood money'. Tom Bell was known as 'the gentleman highwayman' of America. In 1856, he tried to steal gold worth $100,000 from the Marysville **stagecoach**. But guards with guns were hiding on board.

pardon   forgive or excuse someone for a crime

Stand and deliver

John Nevison was a highwayman who was nicknamed Swift Nick. His gang of six **outlaws** usually met at a London **inn** to plan robberies. They shouted 'stand and deliver' as they robbed travellers.

Nevison was famous for making a long journey at great speed to get away from a crime. He once robbed someone in Kent at 4 a.m. but he was recognized. He had to make it look like he was somewhere else so he rode his horse for over 320 kilometres (200 miles). He ended up in York. He changed his clothes and walked through the city to find the **mayor**.

Dick Turpin

Dick Turpin (1705–39) was a famous highwayman. He robbed travellers near London and a large reward was offered to anyone who could catch him. He had to get away fast so he rode to York where he was later arrested for stealing a horse. The police realized who he was and he was hanged.

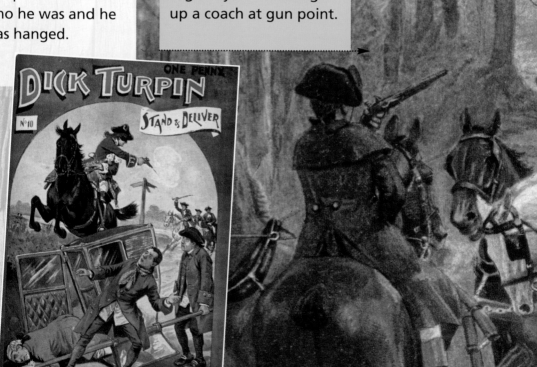

Highwaymen holding up a coach at gun point.

Word Bank   alibi   witness who proves where someone was when a crime took place

Nevison made a bet with the mayor and made a point of pointing to the church clock to say the time was 8 p.m. Later, Nevison was arrested for the robbery in Kent. In his defence, he named the mayor as his **alibi**. How could Nevison rob someone in Kent if he was seen the same day in York? People said it was impossible. He was found not guilty.

Nevison's luck ran out when he was caught for another robbery. He was hanged at York Castle in 1684 at the age of 45. That was old for a highwayman. His body was buried in an unmarked grave.

Black Bess

Dick Turpin was famous for his horse 'Black Bess'. One story told of Turpin's fast ride to York on Black Bess to find an alibi. But like many of the Dick Turpin **legends**, it is untrue. It was John Nevison who made this famous journey.

Bandits of the Wild West

People **migrated** west across the USA in the 19th century. They moved to an area known as the Wild West. It got that name because it was **bandit** country. In the small towns they built, some men lived by their own rules. They had no respect for the law. These **outlaws** ruled with their guns and fast horses. No one was safe.

Everyone knew when the **stagecoach** was coming to town. There might be gold on board. Sometimes it had to slow down as it climbed over rocky hills on dusty tracks far from anywhere. Often there were caves nearby. Just right for waiting inside, ready to pounce. Just right for hiding stolen goods.

The boy bandit

Henry McCarty (below) was born around 1859. He called himself William Bonney. His friends called him Billy. He was very young when he became a robber so he was known as Billy the Kid. He soon became one of the Wild West's most famous outlaws. He killed at least twenty men.

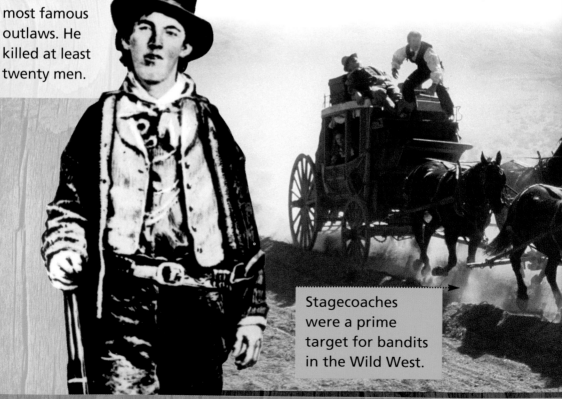

Stagecoaches were a prime target for bandits in the Wild West.

Word Bank

bandit   robber or murderer who is a member of a gang
migrate   move from one area to another

Billy the Kid

At only 12 years old, Billy the Kid killed a man. For the next 10 years he killed and robbed his way around the Wild West. He was caught for another murder when he was 18. He got away by shooting his guards. Once more, no stagecoach was safe.

Pat Garrett

I was the only one to set out to stop Billy the Kid. As the sheriff of Lincoln County, I wanted to get rid of all the outlaws. At last I caught Billy and took him to jail. Once again Billy escaped. It took another year for me to get what I wanted. I shot Billy the Kid dead in 1881.

Pat Garrett

A legend

Billy kept getting away because he had small hands and could slip out of handcuffs. But when he was 21 years old, his luck ran out. Billy was buried at Fort Sumner in New Mexico. You can still see his grave today. Billy the Kid became a **legend**. More than 500 books have been written about him.

REWARD
($5000)
'BILLY THE KID'

Age, 18. Height, 5 feet 3 inches. Weight, 125 lbs. Light hair, blue eyes and even features. He is the leader of the worst band of desperadoes the Territory has ever had to deal with. The above reward will be paid for his capture or positive proof of his death.

JIM DALTON, Sheriff

DEAD OR ALIVE!
'BILLY THE KID'

Plunder on the High Seas

New Orleans

New Orleans in the USA was a base for pirates in the early 1800s. Jean Lafitte was called 'The Gentleman Pirate'. He led 50 ships and more than 1000 pirates from his base on Grand Terre Island. He spoke Spanish, French, Italian and English but was loyal to America by robbing Spanish ships and selling the goods to the people of New Orleans.

Pirates searched for anything valuable – money, jewellery, gold and silver.

In the days when gold and silver were carried across the oceans in sailing ships, there were rich pickings for **outlaws** of the sea – pirates.

Pirate attack

In the dim light of dawn or dusk, a pirate's boat was hard to see. That was when they struck. If a ship did not **surrender** after a warning cannon shot was fired, the pirates used force. They would throw **grappling hooks** on ropes to pull the two ships together and climb aboard with **cutlasses** and pistols. They would kill anyone in their way. Passengers and crew were murdered or taken hostage.

Word Bank   cutlass   short sword with a curved blade

The death penalty

Pirates have been around for more than 3000 years. The main age for pirate attacks on ships was the 18th century, when pirates were called 'outlaws'.

The penalty for being a pirate was a public hanging by the sea. The pirate's body was then hung up in a cage and left to sway in the wind until it rotted away.

Modern pirates

In the 1920s, piracy was a big problem in the Sea of China. One pirate leader was Lai Choi San. He robbed ships and held people to **ransom**. Pirates today use machine guns to steal electrical equipment such as computers from yachts.

Armed gangs today sometimes wait in powerboats to attack luxury yachts at night.

grappling hook   rope with a hook tied to one end, thrown to attach ropes to other ships

Blackbeard

Blackbeard was one of the most feared pirates of all time. He was born in about 1690 in the UK. He became a robber and joined a group of fierce pirates in the Caribbean Sea near Mexico. He later made a base in North Carolina in the USA where he could attack ships travelling along the American coast. Sailors knew they were in deep trouble if they saw Blackbeard's flag flying on a ship. His long black hair and thick beard were a terrifying sight.

Blackbeard once took over a ship sailing out of Charleston. He locked up the passengers and only let them out when they handed over their jewels and clothes.

Warning signs

Pirates often flew flags on their ships. The earliest flags were plain red – the colour of blood. The Jolly Roger flag was black with a white skull and cross-bones. Blackbeard's flag showed a skeleton aiming an arrow at a bleeding heart (above). The hourglass in the other hand meant one thing: the victim's time had run out.

The film *Pirates of the Caribbean* is full of pirate action.

Word Bank   menace   dangerous threat

Fight to the death

It was time for the Royal Navy to get rid of this **menace** of the seas. Captain Robert Maynard was in charge of two naval ships that set out from Virginia in the USA to deal with Blackbeard. After a fierce battle, Maynard and his crew boarded Blackbeard's ship.

With a pistol in one hand and a **cutlass** in the other, Blackbeard came face-to-face with Maynard. They both fired pistols. Blackbeard missed. Maynard did not. In pain, Blackbeard swung his cutlass and snapped off the blade of Maynard's sword. Blackbeard raised his arm for a finishing blow. Just in time, a navy sailor ran up behind Blackbeard and slit his throat.

Another warning

Blackbeard and his gang terrorized the American east coast from 1716 to 1718. In the end, Blackbeard's head was cut off and hung from Maynard's ship (below) as a warning to other pirates. Maynard searched for Blackbeard's hidden treasure but never found it. It could still be out there!

Women pirates

Life on ships in the 18th century was tough. It was hard work, cruel and dangerous. It was a violent man's world – apart from two women who joined the pirate gangs in a search for adventure.

Sailors believed that it was bad luck for women to be on a ship. Any woman wanting to be a sailor had to dress as a man. Anne Bonny did just that when she joined a pirate ship. Her temper soon got her into fights. If any man found out she was a woman, she would cut him down with her sword on the spot.

In disguise

Anne Cormac was born in Ireland in about 1700. Her father took her to America when she was a child. At sixteen she married James Bonny but they soon parted. Now called Anne Bonny, she wanted to escape and start a new life, so she ran away dressed as a man and joined a ship.

An old sketch of Mary Read and Anne Bonny.

Word Bank   convince   make someone believe something

Tough partners

Mary Read was born in London just before 1700. She had a tough childhood. Her parents did not want a girl so they dressed her as a boy. When she grew up, she still dressed as a man and became a soldier. She **convinced** everyone she was a man.

Dressed as a soldier, Mary sailed on a ship. Pirates struck and one of them took Mary back to the pirate ship as a prisoner. The pirate was Anne Bonny. It was only after a while they realized they were both women. They became good friends and sailed together as pirates, getting into fights and killing many men.

Prison

Both Anne Bonny (above) and Mary Read were caught and sent to prison for being pirates. They were due to hang but because they were both pregnant, their lives were spared. However, Mary and her unborn baby died in prison in 1720. No one knows what became of Anne Bonny, or her child.

Trains often carried money and wealthy passengers. Robbing them was a risk. A large gang was needed to rob a train. It took several men to drag a tree or rock on to the track to stop the train.

Railroad robbers in the USA

The Dalton Brothers were four train robbers of the Wild West. Gratton, William, Robert and Emmett often joined up with other **outlaws** to make the job quicker and safer. In 1892, the Dalton Gang tried to rob a train as it came into a station. They saw no lights inside and felt **suspicious**. They let it go. It was just as well because the train was full of armed guards protecting $70,000.

$5000 REWARD

FOR THE CAPTURE

DEAD OR ALIVE

OF

BILL DOOLIN

NOTORIOUS ROBBER OF TRAINS AND BANKS

ABOUT 6 FOOT 2 INCHES TALL, LT. BROWN HAIR, DANGEROUS, ALWAYS HEAVILY ARMED.

Bill Doolin

Born in 1858, Bill Doolin became one of the most famous outlaws of the Wild West. He robbed trains and joined the Dalton Gang on some of their raids. Doolin ended up in jail for robbery but escaped after a few weeks, in a mass break-out of 37 prisoners. In 1896 he was **ambushed** and killed by a **marshal**.

Robbing trains made outlaws rich.

Word Bank

ambush   hide and lie in wait to attack
conviction   proving someone guilty of a crime

Shooting

In their most daring **raid**, eight members of the Dalton Gang held up the Missouri to Texas train. As it came to a halt in a small town, two of the gang climbed into the engine car. The rest went to raid the safe on board.

Unknown to the gang, there were eight guards on the train. A gun battle broke out. Bullets flew through the town as the outlaws galloped off.

REWARD

$5000

for the capture and conviction of each of the **Missouri to Texas train robbers.**

The end of the Daltons

The Dalton Gang once tried to rob two banks at the same time in their hometown of Coffeyville, Kansas. A fierce gun battle killed four citizens and three of the Dalton brothers. Emmett was wounded. He was sentenced to life in prison, but was let out after 14 years. He spent the rest of his days in California.

TIM EVANS   BOB DALTON   GRAT DALTON   DICK BROADWELL

Four of the Dalton Gang lay dead.

Gov. STANFORD

The Wild Bunch

The Wild Bunch had their hideout in the Big Horn Mountains of Wyoming in the USA from 1896 to 1901. Butch Cassidy and The Sundance Kid led the ten or so **outlaws**.

The **payrolls** of mining companies were carried on the Union Pacific Railroad. It was big money. The trains were very slow and the carriages were made out of wood. The Wild Bunch would pick a quiet spot for their attack. They would race their horses beside the train until a rider could jump on board while another grabbed his horse.

Once on the train, the robber would unhitch the carriages from the engine and they would blow the safe open with dynamite.

Tricks of the trade

Some outlaws would travel as passengers on trains. When they reached a certain spot, they took control. Waiting gang members would jump on to the train and rob the passengers or steal **cargo**. Railroads began to use faster trains with trained gunmen and powerful rifles on board. That put a stop to railroad robberies.

Paul Newman and Robert Redford act as Butch Cassidy and The Sundance Kid in the 1969 film.

Word Bank   payroll   money paid in cash to workers

With a bang

In 1899 the Wild Bunch went extra wild on the Union Pacific Railroad. They unhitched a carriage and lit the fuse on the dynamite. The whole carriage blew up. They survived but they still had not managed to open the safe. They lit more dynamite and this time the whole safe blew up, throwing money all over the track.

As the wind blew dollar notes into the air, the gang had to scramble all over the place to pick them up. Even so, they escaped with $30,000.

The last known train robbery by Wild Bunch outlaws took place in Montana in 1901. They escaped with $40,500 from the Great Northern Railroad.

A happy ending

A reward of $3000 was offered to anyone who would bring in Butch Cassidy and The Sundance Kid, dead or alive. So they had to leave the country with their hoard of $30,000. Using false names, Butch and The Kid bought a cattle ranch in South America. They started new lives as farmers and were never caught.

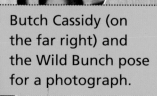

Butch Cassidy (on the far right) and the Wild Bunch pose for a photograph.

England's Great Train Robbery

On 8 August 1963, the Glasgow to London train was packed with mailbags containing £2.6 million. At 3 a.m. masked robbers struck. The gang covered a green railway light and shone a red torch to stop the train. They knocked out the driver and unloaded 128 mail sacks, rushing them to a hide-out at a farm nearby.

The plan was to lie low, then move the money before cleaning away all the clues. But the men hired to clean up did not do their job. When the police found the farm they also found fingerprints. Before long the whole gang was behind bars.

Train-raiders

It was called 'the robbery of the century'. The seventeen members of the gang kept £90,000 each. But the police found some of the money, as well as all the gang. They were soon serving 30-year prison sentences.

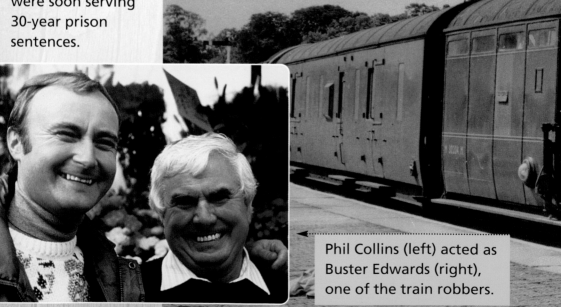

Phil Collins (left) acted as Buster Edwards (right), one of the train robbers.

Word Bank   rogue   dishonest person who is often up to mischief

A modern-day outlaw

Ronnie Biggs was a key member of the gang. In 1965, after 15 months in prison, he climbed a wall and escaped. Friends helped him get to Australia and then to Brazil where he lived as a hero. Many people saw him as just a lovable **rogue**.

Biggs avoided getting caught for the next 35 years. In 2001, Biggs had enough of life as an **outlaw**. He was a sick old man and wanted to go home. He returned to England but the police were waiting. They took him back to prison to end his days behind bars. He had 28 years left to serve.

A star criminal

The train robber Ronnie Biggs was 34 on the day of the robbery. He spent the second half of his life in Brazil, where he became a famous citizen. The British police could not arrest him in Brazil. His rich lifestyle made him a celebrity and he even acted in a film.

The carriage robbed by the train robbers.

Hand over the money

Armed robbery was a risky way to steal large amounts of money.

Bank robbers of the Wild West

Banks in the Wild West were very tempting to **outlaws**. Robbers would sweep into town in a cloud of dust, shooting and yelling. A small bank would not stand a chance. The masked gang would grab all the money and leave in minutes. They did not care if they shot anyone.

The James Gang

Frank James and his younger brother Jesse led a violent gang of outlaws. Everyone feared the James Gang. Some of their **raids** used over twelve men. Their first raid was in Missouri in 1866. It was the first daylight bank robbery in America. The James Gang got rich but they still wanted more.

The rule of fear

Why did these outlaws bring so much terror? Why did the banks hand over all their money? The answer is simple: guns. **Bandits** shot anything that moved. They did not care who got hurt. They used guns called six shooters (right). These guns could fire six bullets before being reloaded. Nobody argued with one of those.

Never trust an outlaw

There was a reward of $10,000 for anyone who could catch Jesse James: dead or alive. Robert Ford was one of Jesse's gang and he wanted this prize. In 1882 he went into Jesse's house. He raised his gun and fired. Jesse James fell to the ground with a bullet in the back of his head. He was just 34.

No reward

Robert Ford never got the reward money. Later he was killed in a bar fight. One thing seems true about outlaws – they did not live to enjoy old age.

Jesse James

Jesse robbed his first bank when he was 18. Over the next 16 years, he and his gang robbed many banks. They left 14 people dead. Some of Jesse's gang were shot too, but there were always more outlaws who wanted to join the famous James Gang.

Jesse James in his coffin in 1882.

A rough start

Charles Floyd (above) was born in 1904, one of seven children. Life was tough. He married when he was 17. He bought his first gun at the age of 18 and held up a post office for $350. Although he was arrested, his father gave him an **alibi**.

Pretty Boy Floyd

The 1920s and 1930s were hard times in America because there was little work or money. Some people took to crime to pay their bills. Charles Floyd started his life of crime in Ohio. The first person he killed was a police officer who stopped him robbing a bank in 1931. Other **outlaws** hired him and his machine gun for different robbery jobs.

During the next 17 months, Floyd was hunted by every police force in the country. A $23,000 'dead or alive' reward was offered and many called him Public Enemy Number One.

Word Bank   black market   criminals buying or selling illegal goods

Full time crook

Some people saw Floyd as a hero like Robin Hood. They called him 'the people's **bandit**' because he stole from banks to buy food for the poor. This is probably just a **legend**.

In 1934, Floyd was **identified** as one of three men who robbed a bank in Ohio. The next day the police shot at two **suspects** carrying guns. One was caught but Floyd escaped. Three days later the police shot him dead when he tried to run away through a forest. Floyd's body was put in a funeral home where 10,000 people came to visit in three hours. He was famous even in death.

Tough times

In 1929, the New York stock market collapsed and left many people poor and out of work. This time was called the Great Depression. In the following years, 1930s America was a good time for gangsters and outlaws. Many criminals sold whisky on the **black market**. Machine guns, cars and smart suits were now common for outlaws.

John Ericson played the part of Floyd in a film.

suspect   someone thought to be responsible for a crime

Bonnie and Clyde

Bonnie Parker was 20 years old when she met Clyde Barrow in Dallas, Texas, in 1930. He was 2 years older than her and a real **rebel**. For both of them it was love at first sight. They became partners in crime, too.

Before long they were robbing and killing their way across six states. Together they became front-page news across the country. Clyde was a master gunman. He was the leader of the Barrow Gang. They were feared for robbing banks, shops and filling stations. They killed whoever got in their way, including police officers.

Partners in crime

From the time Bonnie and Clyde met, they only had 4 years and 4 months left to live. This was a tragic love story. During their time together, Bonnie and Clyde (below) were **accused** of killing at least twelve men.

From the film *Bonnie and Clyde*.

Word Bank

accuse   blame someone for doing wrong
FBI   Federal Bureau of Investigation of America

The hunt

The **FBI** organized one of the biggest manhunts America had ever seen. One by one, members of the Barrow Gang were caught. But not Bonnie and Clyde. They kept one step ahead. But their luck would have to run out soon. The net began to close in when the police found out where they were staying.

On 23 May 1934, Bonnie and Clyde drove straight in to a trap in Gibsland, Louisiana. Police hiding in the nearby bushes **ambushed** them. In 12 seconds, 167 bullets slammed in to their car with at least 50 bullets tearing into Bonnie and Clyde. They both died instantly.

The car Bonnie and Clyde were shot and killed in.

Side by side

Bonnie knew how their story would end. It was just a matter of time. She wrote a short poem soon before the police shot them.

Someday they'll go down together;
And they'll bury us side by side;
To few it'll be grief –
To the law a relief –
But it's death for Bonnie and Clyde.

Livestock thieves

Some robbers chose not to steal money. Instead they stole valuable **livestock**.

Horse thieves

Horse theft was a serious crime and many horse thieves were hanged. They were rated as 'no good, dirty, rotten **scoundrels'** because many men rated their horses as their most important possessions.

Round them up

In the Wild West, many cowboys looked after herds of cattle that roamed freely through vast open areas. These cowboys could not be everywhere at once to keep their eyes on their animals.

It was hardly surprising that some **outlaws** tried their hand at stealing cattle. Stealing and selling cattle could make them money fast. Even so, many thieves found robbing banks was easier.

Most outlaws turned away from rustling when cattle ranchers hired 'Range Detectives'. These men made life much harder for the rustlers. Making a fast getaway with a herd of cattle was difficult.

A good horse was very important to a man's work in the Wild West.

Word Bank   **livestock**   horses, cattle, sheep and other animals kept on a farm

Belle Starr

There were not many women outlaws in the Wild West. But one became known as 'the Bandit Queen'. Maybelle Shirley was born in 1848. When she married Samuel Starr, a Native American, she became Belle Starr. She also became a horse thief and a murderer.

Belle went to live in the Indian Territory in Oklahoma, in the USA where her home became a safe place for outlaws. In 1883, she was sent to prison for horse-stealing. On her release, she was back in the saddle but she, too, ended up like so many outlaws. An unknown person shot her dead. A book *Belle Starr, the Bandit Queen* was later written about her amazing life.

Keeping it in the family

Belle Starr (below) had a nephew called Henry Starr, a thief who spent years in prison. He was first arrested for horse theft but started robbing banks in 1893. He went on to become the first bank robber to use a car in a bank robbery in 1921.

Stealing cattle was called 'rustling'.

THE BANDIT QUEEN OR THE FEMALE JESSE JAMES

HANDSOMELY AND PROFUSELY ILLUSTRATED PRICE 25¢

Australian bushrangers

Through most of the 1800s, bushrangers roamed the **outback** of Australia. Many were men who had just been released from prison. They had nowhere to go. Stealing sheep helped them to survive. Some bushrangers joined large gangs and moved on to robbing farms and banks.

New South Wales was good sheep country. **Settlers** came to build up large **sheep stations**. In the early 1800s, about 80 per cent of the population were **ex-convicts**. Many of them started by stealing animals. Then by joining gangs, bushrangers turned to bigger crimes and even murder. **Outlaws** in the outback got out of control.

Convicts

Thousands of criminals were **deported** from Britain to Australia in the early 1800s. Even if they were allowed back to Britain, they could never afford the fare home. So when they were released from prison, many ex-convicts joined together to become outlaw gangs. They **raided** sheep farms, cattle stations and horse stables.

From the 2003 film *Ned Kelly*.

Word Bank

deported   sent away to another country
ex-convict   person who has been released from prison

Ned Kelly

Ned Kelly's father arrived in Australia as a convict from Ireland. He stole a cow and went back to prison. He died when Ned was 11 in 1866.
By the age of 23, Ned had his own horse-stealing business, but it did not make enough money.

With his brother Dan and two other outlaws, Ned began to rob banks. When he shot and killed three policemen in 1878, the Government declared the Kelly Gang to be outlaws. Two years later, the police finally tracked them down.

Dressed in home-made armour, the Kelly Gang came out to face the bullets. Ned was shot in the leg and arrested. He was hanged in Old Melbourne **Gaol** aged 25 years old.

They died young

Ned Kelly (above) became a famous figure in Australian **folktales** and is shown as a hero in some films. Hundreds of other bushrangers are forgotten – after coming to an unhappy end.

'Bold' Jack Donahue – shot dead in 1830 aged 23

'Jackey Jackey' Westwood – hanged in 1846 aged 27

Matthew Brady – hanged in 1826 aged 27

Ben Hall – shot dead in 1865 aged 28

Fred Ward – shot dead in 1870 aged 35

outback   Australia's wild country, far from towns
settler   someone who 'settles' to live in a new country

Pancho Villa

General Porfirio Díaz ruled Mexico for 30 years. By 1910, many **peasants** were fed-up with him because he did not seem to care about them. They wanted someone else to run the country but the President would not let anyone take over. The people plotted to get rid of him. One of the plotters was a well-known **outlaw** called Pancho Villa.

Pancho led a **bandit** army in north Mexico. He was already a wanted outlaw in America because he kept crossing the border into Texas to steal cattle.

Wanted

Pancho Villa was born in Mexico in 1878. He was seen as a hero by the poor but as a cruel outlaw by many others. Some saw him as a violent Robin Hood who sometimes helped the poor. Pancho's first murder **victim** was a man who attacked his sister. He became a wanted man for many crimes.

Word Bank

assassinate   kill a leader for political reasons
peasant   poor farm-worker

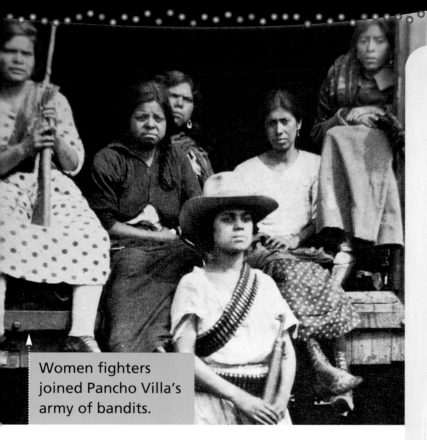

Women fighters joined Pancho Villa's army of bandits.

Forgiven

A new political group wanted both Pancho Villa (below) and his power out of the way. They **assassinated** him in 1923, when Pancho was aged 45. More than 40 years later, the Mexican Congress wrote his name in gold on the chamber walls with other heroes of the Mexican Revolution. A cattle-rustling outlaw had become **respectable**.

The people's hero

Pancho Villa was very popular with Mexico's poor people. He was not popular with Texan farmers who lost herds of cattle to his gangs. He hid from the American and Mexican armies for 10 years, surviving by stealing cattle. Neither army could catch him.

Pancho's battle to get rid of the President meant his army of bandits had to attack the country's soldiers. The fighting lasted a few months until the President was forced to leave in 1911. Pancho was a hero of the **revolution**. He made a deal with the new government and gave up his guns in exchange for land.

respectable   honest and decent
revolution   defeating a government by force

Lawmen of the Wild West

One of the reasons why the Wild West was so unlawful was that there was no organized police force. Cowboys often took the law into their own hands and shot at men they thought might be **outlaws**. A town's **sheriff** would try to keep law and order but some sheriffs were dishonest. They just wanted power – and the excuse to shoot at anyone they chose.

Lawman of legend

Wild Bill Hickok (above) lived from 1837 to 1876. His fast-shooting made him famous. He even toured with Buffalo Bill's Wild West Show in 1872. Television programmes and films have shown him as a brave outlaw-hunter. In real life he probably broke the law several times himself.

Word Bank   saloon   drinking bar

Wild Bill Hickok

James Hickok was born in Illinois in America. He soon learned to shoot a gun very fast. He was called 'Wild Bill' because of his quick temper. He was also well known for gambling, but he became a town **marshal** in Kansas in 1869.

Fast shooter

Before Hickok became a marshal, he had a job driving a **stagecoach**. Outlaws sometimes attacked him, so he learned how to look after himself. He became ready to take them on.

The McCanles outlaw gang was wanted for train robbery, murder, bank robbery, cattle rustling and horse theft. Hickok heard that they had set up a camp nearby. He liked a good fight and there was reward money, too. He was determined to get them.

Wild Bill Hickok took on the entire McCanles gang single-handed. He killed Jeb McCanles and two of his men, and took the rest as prisoners. He collected a $175 reward.

Fights between cowboys often got out of control.

Revenge

Jack McCall entered a **saloon** in Deadwood, South Dakota, where Wild Bill Hickok was playing a game of poker. Hickok had killed Jack's brother in Kansas. Under his coat, McCall's hand was on his pistol. He shot Hickok in the back of the head, killing him instantly. Hickok was just 39. McCall was later hanged.

The OK Corral

When the railroad reached Dodge City, Kansas in 1872, it was bad news for the town.
It became a centre for buffalo hunters and wild cowboys. Crime levels exploded.

The local **cemetery** was called Boot Hill because so many men died with their boots on in gunfights. Someone was needed to keep law and order.

Wyatt Earp arrived in Dodge City in 1878. He could draw his gun quickly and was a sharp shooter. He soon became assistant **marshal** and dealt with the **outlaws** of Dodge City, before moving on to Tombstone in Arizona where his three brothers lived.

The gunfighters

Wyatt Earp was a **saloon** keeper in Tombstone, Arizona (below) at the time of the famous gunfight at the OK Corral. His brother Virgil Earp was the **sheriff**. He made Wyatt, Morgan Earp and their friend Doc Holliday marshals just in time for the fight with the Clanton and McLaury Gangs.

Word Bank   cemetery   graveyard for burying the dead

Guns blazing

In 1880 the Earp brothers had a row with two families, the Clantons and the McLaurys.

Wyatt Earp **accused** the Clanton brothers of stealing his horse. At the OK **Corral** he told Billy Clanton and Frank McLaury to hand over their guns. Billy Clanton fired at Wyatt Earp. He missed and Morgan Earp fired twice. Billy Clanton fell back against a wall. A bullet hit Frank McLaury in the stomach and he fell to the ground. Tom McLaury tried to run but was gunned down. All three men lay dead. More guns fired and men fell hurt. With the gunfight over, the only man unhurt was Wyatt Earp.

A town with the name of death

Tombstone had a bad name for drink and death. The small town had more than twenty saloons. Wyatt Earp (above) moved away from Tombstone to Los Angeles, where he died in 1929 at the age of 80. Lawmen tended to live longer than outlaws!

Would you argue with these men?

corral   fenced pen for keeping cattle or horses in

Fighting back: Bill Cody

This hero of the Wild West was not so much a lawman as a good citizen who fought off several **outlaws**. At 14 years old, Bill Cody became a rider on the famous Pony Express. It was a dangerous route, with outlaws and Native Americans likely to attack at any time. Once, he was nearly captured by a band of outlaws.

On another journey, outlaws killed the rider who was meant to take over from Bill Cody. He had to ride another 136 kilometres (85 miles) before turning back. This was one of the longest rides in the history of the Pony Express – 518 kilometres (322 miles) in 21 hours.

Pony Express

The Pony Express (above) was set up in 1860 as a fast mail service. The riders received a Bible, a pair of guns and $125 a month. They had to ride at high speed through dangerous country from the Mid West to California. Stations were 64 to 160 kilometres (40 to 100 miles) apart – with lots of outlaws in between!

Poster from 1899 for Buffalo Bill's show.

Word Bank reputation   what people believe about a person's character

Buffalo Bill

Bill Cody became known as Buffalo Bill. In 1883 he ran his famous Buffalo Bill Wild West Show, touring through America and Europe. He tried to show that there was more to the Wild West than just ruthless outlaws. He died in 1917 at the age of 70. It was yet more proof that law-keepers outlived law-breakers.

Shows like Buffalo Bill's reminded the world that the Wild West needed strong characters to enforce the law. This has always been the case in all parts of the world. Without proper rules and the right people to police them, crime takes over. That is when the outlaws rule.

Hang 'em high

Roy Bean was a judge who sentenced many outlaws by saying, 'Hang 'em first, try 'em later'. He had a **reputation** for giving outlaws harsh sentences. They gave him the name, 'The Hangin' Judge'. Another **legend** tells of Judge Isaac Parker of Arkansas. He sentenced 172 men to execution and even hanged 88 of them himself!

Roy Bean's shack.

43

Find out more

In hiding

A Romanian man hid in his basement to avoid an 8 year prison sentence. He had been charged with trying to kill his neighbour. A friend who was helping him with food supplies finally decided to tell police where he was – 11 years after the original sentence!

If you want to find out more about the criminal underworld, why not have a look at these books:

Behind the Scenes: Solving a Crime, Peter Mellet (Heinemann Library, 1999)

Forensic Files: Investigating Murders, Paul Dowswell (Heinemann Library, 2004)

Forensic Files: Investigating Thefts and Heists, Alex Woolf (Heinemann Library, 2004)

Just the Facts: Cyber Crime, Neil McIntosh (Heinemann Library, 2002)

Did you know?

In Australia it is a crime in some states to:

- own a mattress without a mattress licence
- wear pink hot pants after midday on Sundays
- change a light bulb unless you are an electrician!

Criminal records

- The world's first speeding ticket was issued in the UK in 1896 to a man called Walter Arnold. He was travelling at 8 mph in a 2 mph zone.

- The most successful sniffer dog was a Labrador from the USA called Snag. He found 118 different hoards of hidden drugs worth an amazing £580 million!

- The oldest person to be hanged was 82 year old Allan Mair in 1843. He was hanged in the UK sitting down because he was unable to stand.

- The world's largest safe-deposit-box robbery took place in 1976. A group of highly-trained criminals stole more than £22 million worth of goods from a bank in the Middle East.

Robin Hood

A festival takes place every year in Nottingham to celebrate the life of the famous **outlaw**, Robin Hood. During the festival, jugglers and jesters roam the streets. **Archers** compete in full medieval costume and a competition is held to find the best Robin Hood look-alike!

Glossary

accuse blame someone for doing wrong

alibi witness who proves where someone was when a crime took place

ambush hide and lie in wait to attack

archer person who fights with a bow and arrow

assassinate kill a leader for political reasons

bandit robber or murderer who is a member of a gang

betray tell tales on someone and get them into trouble

black market criminals buying or selling illegal goods

cargo goods carried on a train, plane or ship

cemetery graveyard for burying the dead

conviction proving someone guilty of a crime

convince make someone believe something

corral fenced pen for keeping cattle or horses in

cutlass short sword with a curved blade

deported sent away to another country

ex-convict person who has been released from prison

FBI Federal Bureau of Investigation of America

fiction made-up story

folktale old story told over generations

gaol jail

grappling hook rope with a hook tied to one end, thrown to attach ropes to other ships

identify recognize

inn resting house for travellers, where they could eat and sleep overnight

legend story based on something real that may not be completely true

livestock horses, cattle, sheep and other animals kept on a farm

marshal officer of the law

mayor person in charge of running a town or city

menace dangerous threat

migrate move from one area to another

notorious well known for something bad

outback Australia's wild country, far from towns

outlaw robber on the run, wanted by the law enforcers

pardon forgive or excuse someone for a crime

payroll money paid in cash to workers

peasant poor farm-worker

raid sudden attack

ransom payment demanded for the release of a prisoner

rebel person who fights against authority

reputation what people believe about a person's character

respectable honest and decent

revolution defeating a government by force

rogue dishonest person who is often up to mischief

saloon drinking bar

scoundrel villain

settler someone who 'settles' to live in a new country

sheep station large sheep farm

sheriff local law chief who kept peace and order

stagecoach wagon pulled by horses from town to town

surrender give in to someone else's control

suspect someone thought to be responsible for a crime

suspicious suspecting that something wrong is happening

victim someone who is affected by crime

villain criminal or evil person

western story or film set in the Wild West of America

Index